Welcome to
I SPY
Valentine's
Day
GOOD LUCK!

See if you can guess all
the puzzles correctly
in this fun book!

I SPY with my little eye, something beginning with...

A is for

Arrow

I SPY with my little eye, something beginning with...

B is for

Balloons

I SPY with my little eye, something beginning with...

C is for

Cake

I SPY with my little eye, something beginning with...

D is for

Doves

I SPY with my little eye, something beginning with...

E is for

Envelope

I SPY with my little eye, something beginning with...

F

is for

Flowers

I SPY with my little eye, something beginning with...

G

is for

Gift

I SPY with my little eye, something beginning with...

H is for

Heart

I SPY with my little eye, something beginning with...

K is for

Key

I SPY with my little eye, something beginning with...

C is for

Chocolate

I SPY with my little eye, something beginning with...

D is for

Donuts

I SPY with my little eye, something beginning with...

F is for

February

I SPY with my little eye, something beginning with...

C is for

Cupid

I SPY with my little eye, something beginning with...

K is for

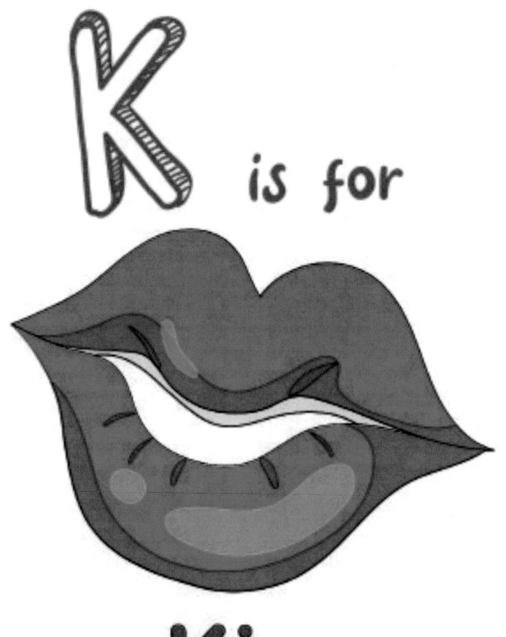

Kiss

I SPY with my little eye, something beginning with...

R is for

Ring

I SPY with my little eye, something beginning with...

C is for

Cupcake

I SPY with my little eye, something beginning with...

R

is for

Rose

I SPY with my little eye, something beginning with...

M is for

Mailbox

I SPY with my little eye, something beginning with...

T

is for

Teddy bear

Made in the USA
Las Vegas, NV
03 February 2021